DETROIT PUBLIC LIBRARY

3 5674 02366850 3

DETROIT PUBLIC LIBRARY

HUBBARD BRANCH LIBRARY
12929 W. McNICHOLS
DETROIT, MICHIGAN 48235

DATE DUE

OCT 1 9 1995

JAN 2 4 1996

BC-3

D1064160

jB

B;P662R

THE TRIAL
OF JOHN BROWN

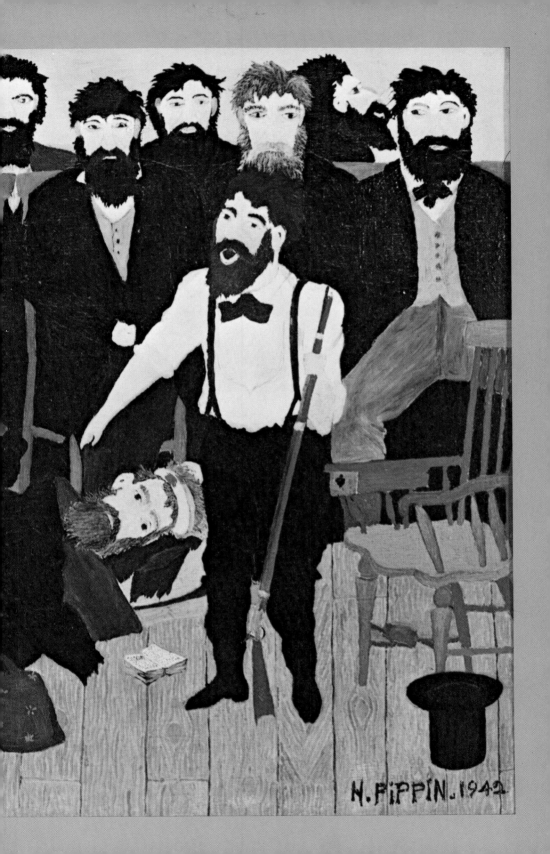

H. PiPPiN. 1942

Front end paper: THE TRIAL OF JOHN BROWN (1942) Courtesy of American Heritage Publishing Co., Inc.

Back end paper: THE HOLY MOUNTAIN III (1945) Lent by the Joseph H. Hirshhorn Collection

HORACE PIPPIN

THE ARTIST AS A BLACK AMERICAN

SELDEN RODMAN & CAROLE CLEAVER

DOUBLEDAY & COMPANY, INC., GARDEN CITY, NEW YORK

jB

P662R

c. 2

JAN '77

Library of Congress Catalog Card Number 76–175397

Copyright © 1972 by Selden Rodman

All Rights Reserved

Printed in the United States of America

First Edition

Frontis: PORTRAIT OF HORACE PIPPIN, From the book *Horace Pippin, A Negro Painter in America,* by Selden Rodman. Copyright 1947 by the Quadrangle Press, Inc. Reprinted by permission of Selden Rodman.

Jacket photo: SELF PORTRAIT (1941) Lent by Albright-Knox Art Gallery, Buffalo, New York.

TO JACOB LAWRENCE

"Diversity is the word. Let man keep his many parts
and you'll have no tyrant states. Why, if they
follow this conformity business they'll end up by
forcing me, an invisible man, to become white,
which is not a color but a lack of one."

—RALPH ELLISON

ACKNOWLEDGMENTS

We wish to express our thanks for help in preparing this book first and foremost to Robert Carlen of Philadelphia, Mr. and Mrs. Richard F. Wade of West Chester, and Leon Arkus, Director of the Carnegie Institute's Museum in Pittsburgh.

Also to Mr. Percy Raymond, Mr. Edward Valentine, Mr. Joseph Fuggett, Miss Emma F. Milby, Mrs. Carita Ponzo, Miss Pauline Loper, and Mr. Rodney Loper of West Chester; and to Mr. and Mrs. John Bruyn, Mr. William Walsh of the *Evening News*, both of Goshen, New York; and to the Honorable Paul Dague, former Congressman from Chester County, Pennsylvania; and to Drs. Michael McGuire and Frank Kaplan at the Norristown State Hospital.

Also to Mr. and Mrs. David Grossman and Mr. and Mrs. Samuel Feldman of Philadelphia; Mr. and Mrs. William Cleaver of Paoli; Miss Violette de Mazia of the Barnes Foundation in Merion; and to the art and photographic staffs of the Philadelphia *Inquirer*.

Also to Mr. and Mrs. Nathan Alexander of Gladwynne,

Pennsylvania; Mrs. Okey Chenoweth, Mrs. Philip Filippone and Mrs. Maia Wojciechowska of Oakland, New Jersey.

Also to Andrew Wyeth and John McCoy of Chadds Ford, Pennsylvania. And to Lee A. Ault of New York City, publisher of the original Pippin monograph by Selden Rodman.

Books that proved especially helpful to us include Elizabeth Sharts's *Land o' Goshen*, Emmett J. Scott's *Official History of the American Negro in the World War*, Florette Henri's *Bitter Victory*, Stephen Oates's biography of John Brown, *To Purge This Land with Blood*, Frederick C. Wight's *Milestones of American Painting*, Henry Hart's *Albert C. Barnes: A Tribute*, and *Argyrol King: The Life and Times of Albert C. Barnes*.

LIST OF ILLUSTRATIONS

Color Illustrations

9

INTRODUCTION

Like all the great self-taught or "popular" artists—Henri Rousseau and Camile Bombois of France; Philomé Obin and Georges Liautaud of Haiti; Asilia Guillén of Nicaragua; John Kane and Clara Williamson in the United States—Horace Pippin was a late bloomer. Why this is so is a mystery. In some cases, Pippin's among them, it may have been a matter of belated discovery. Artists too poor to go to art schools or to acquire friends in the affluent art world depend for their recognition on the happy accident of being "discovered" by the sophisticated or the rich. And in many cases, surely, they are never discovered at all. In other cases, the opportunity to devote themselves to their art may only come late in life. But the mystery remains.

Horace Pippin's discovery—by the Pennsylvania art critic Christian Brinton and the famous illustrator N. C. Wyeth—came in the forty-ninth year of his life, when he had only just begun to paint. In the nine years that were left to him Pippin painted all but one of his important pictures, was exhibited in the Museum of Modern Art, was given half a dozen one-man shows, was collected greedily by connoisseurs in the Philadelphia and New York areas, and enjoyed considerable fame. In the year of his death work was begun on a sumptuously illustrated monograph, *Horace Pippin: A Negro Artist in America* by Selden Rodman, and the book was published the following year with a catalogue of the artist's known works. It quickly went out of print, and in the two decades that followed Horace Pippin's reputation suffered something of an eclipse. Then a revival of interest began. Museums, including the Metropolitan of New York, began acquiring the few of his pictures still available. The Carnegie Institute of Pittsburgh mounted a splendid exhibition and printed a lavish catalogue. At an auction one minor picture was sold for a sum of money exceeding everything that the artist had earned in a lifetime. The time had come for a book about Horace Pippin that would gather together all those available facts relating to his life which were beyond the scope of the original monograph.

Lest it be too late . . . and it almost was. There were friends and relatives, a very few, who still remembered Horace Pippin. There were archives to be consulted, birth and death records, Veterans Administration files, to be added to the scant account of his life given by the artist in his *Autobiography* and *War Diaries* included in the monograph. The towns of Goshen, New York, and West Chester, Pennsylvania, scenes of Pippin's obscure youth and triumphant last years, had happily changed very little. But if Mr. Peter Hyun, editor of Books for Young Readers Department at Doubleday & Company, had not come forward at this juncture the present biography might never have been undertaken. Thanks above all are due to him.

Long before it was acknowledged that "Black is beautiful" and that "Afro-Americans" had created a culture of their own in the United States, Horace Pippin had unself-consciously celebrated these self-evident truths in his paintings—unself-consciously because in the time and circumstances in which he lived, only a handful of intellectuals had formulated such concepts. Pippin's pride in being black is manifested in all his work. And in many of his best pictures his pride in being a part of his race's heroic struggle out of slavery and toward self-fulfillment is just as manifest. But these were not feelings Pippin expressed aggressively because they were only part of his pride in being an American. . .

In the period of the two world wars, and the years between them, most black Americans felt this way, for better or for worse, and Horace Pippin was no exception. Probably he had never heard of Christus Attucks, or Nat Turner, or even Frederick Douglass; but John Brown and Abraham Lincoln were among his heroes—for what he believed to be their roles in freeing his people from slavery. Had he been asked who the great Americans of his own time were, he no doubt would have answered: Woodrow Wilson and Franklin Roosevelt. Racial prejudice he must have encountered—in Goshen, in West Chester, above all in the segregated Army of World War I—but prejudice seems to have left him unscarred and unresentful. Like most blacks of that day he believed in the American Dream: his people would achieve full equality in American society by dint of their own efforts, with a little help from their (white) friends. Didn't the Declaration of Independence, the Constitution, and the Emancipation Proclamation guarantee it?

MR. PREJUDICE, the only picture with an overt racial message that Horace Pippin ever painted, was undoubtedly inspired by those white friends among his patrons and collectors who were militants. There was nothing in the picture's condemnation of Klansmen and such that he wouldn't have subscribed to as a matter of course. But it was a political poster, not the kind of brooding memory of the joys and sorrows of his people that inspired his best pictures. It would be very easy to interpret the four HOLY MOUNTAIN pictures—the black child gamboling among the carnivorous beasts, the black Isaiah presiding over the peaceful assemblage out of which the white lion and pig stare sullenly—as racial parables. Too easy. Horace Pippin had seen modern war at its most grisly, had been the first to paint its horrors convincingly, and hoped in all the goodness of his simple heart that there would never be another such holocaust. But there is nothing in his war diaries to indicate that he regarded the American contribution to World War I as anything but a necessary effort on the part of blacks and whites alike; or that the camaraderie, heroism, and suffering he experienced in France were not accepted by him as the most memorable year of an otherwise uneventful life.

14

Mr. Prejudice (1943) Owned by Dr. and Mrs. Matthew T. Moore

Was Horace Pippin a "great painter" in the accepted canon of Western art, or only a "talented primitive"?

It is our opinion that his best pictures—like the best of Rousseau and a very few others among the self-taught—fall somewhere between these two categories. Lacking the technical virtuosity and inventive ambition of High Art, these "naïve" painters, nevertheless, by their intuitive grasp of the principles of composition, color, and accommodation to the flatness of the picture-plane, achieve the same quality of timelessness as the Masters. There is the same sense of arrested mobility; the same transformation of the humble into the noble, the here-and-now into forever. In academic painting, which busies itself with surface resemblances, this never happens. *Content* (the subject, the message) is not deeply felt, and therefore one is conscious only of the artist's skill. But the Brueghels and the Pippins share one thing in common: everything is subordinated to the unfolding of a vision, the creation of a world.

Inevitably Pippin was deflected from this goal from time to time. He was an impressionable man, and much too good-natured not to take advice (often bad advice) from well-meaning friends and critics. He painted his share of picture postcards. And he didn't have Alain Locke to tell him that Winslow Homer—who painted his own share of picture postcards, and with a sentimentality Pippin was incapable of—had broken the "cotton-patch-and-back-porch tradition" once and for all in THE GULF STREAM, the painting that marked in Locke's words "the artistic emancipation of the Negro in American art." But instinctively Pippin returned to the world he knew: the world of nature, the world of Goshen and his mother's memories, the world of West Chester, the world of impoverished, hard-working, suffering and enduring blacks that needed no ideology to make it real, no prettifying to make it palatable.

In such great pictures as SHELL HOLES AND OBSERVATION BALLOON, THE GET-AWAY, DOMINO PLAYERS, SUNDAY MORNING BREAKFAST, THE BARRACKS, THE PARK BENCH, the John Brown trio and the Holy Mountain quartet, and the final small, glowing flower pieces, Horace Pippin bequeathed a world to his people, and to all of us.

It was warm in the big farmhouse kitchen, and Jim Gavin was tired after his long day's work. While his wife washed the dishes and his children frolicked on the floor with his hired boy, Horace Pippin, Jim's eyes blinked a few times and then closed. He was soon sound asleep, sitting straight up in his chair.

Mrs. Gavin finished her clean-up and bundled the children off to bed. Fourteen-year-old Horace stared for some moments at Gavin's sleeping face. Then, finding a scrap of paper, he sat down and began to sketch, transferring Gavin's craggy features to the paper.

Mrs. Gavin returned to the kitchen, and with the sudden noise Jim awoke. He smiled sheepishly at Horace. "I musta dozed off."

"Yessir."

Gavin rose heavily from his chair and shuffled toward the fire. "What's this?" he asked, noticing the picture. "Who made it?"

"I did."

"Why, it's not bad at all," said Gavin, taking another

look. "I can hardly believe you did it. You ought to go to art school!"

"I'd like that," Horace said, "but I don't reckon I ever will."

"Well, you should," Gavin said. "You must. I'll see to it. I'll write some letters first thing in the morning."

Horace's face expanded in a smile. "I'd *like* that," he said. "I sure would like that." He got his things together and prepared to go to his room above the stable.

It certainly would be something, wouldn't it now? It certainly would be something if he, Horace Pippin, could go to a real art school, and learn how to do it all just right. It would be worth all the whippings he'd gotten for drawing when he should have been doing his school work. It would be worth—well, it would be worth just about anything.

He started across the barnyard, and just as he was nearing the stable he heard a voice.

"Pssst, Horace . . ."

"Who's that?"

"It's me, John."

Horace watched his younger brother emerge from the shadows. "John, what you doin' here?"

"I come to get you," said John. "Ma's sick. She's real sick. She say you'll have to get a job in Goshen now, so you can look after her some, after hours."

"Where I gonna get a job in Goshen?"

"Oh, there's lotsa jobs. Man at the feed store needs a boy, and they're puttin' on a lotta folks down at the coalyard."

"But Mr. Gavin, he—"

"He what?"

"Nothin'."

John followed Horace up the stairs to his room. "You better get your things together so we can leave soon as it's light."

"OK," Horace said, "but what's wrong with Ma? She ain't gonna die, is she?"

"I don't know nothin' about it," John said.

Horace began to stuff his things into a feed sack. "I gotta see her. I gotta see her," he said, the art school forgotten.

At that moment it seemed very unlikely that Horace Pippin would become one of America's finest artists.

Horace Pippin was born February 22, 1888 in West Chester, Pennsylvania, just twenty-five years after the Civil War and less than twenty miles from the South. His grandparents had been born slaves and his grandmother had witnessed the hanging of John Brown, the white abolitionist whose attack on the federal arsenal at Harpers Ferry had touched off the Civil War.

When Horace was three his parents took him and his baby brother, John, to Goshen, New York, where they found work as domestics. At Goshen the Pippins moved into a two-story frame house at 339 West Main Street, less than a quarter of a mile from the center of town. There his mother, Christine Pippin, saw to it that the children said their prayers, read the Bible, and learned to play the old-fashioned "Century" organ that dominated the front room.

Goshen, a village of 3500, considered itself a progressive town, for it was both the county seat and the place chosen by the Erie Railroad for its terminal. Men of Goshen had fought and died in the Civil War to stamp out slavery. Even so, Goshen's schools were segregated.

Horace attended the one-room "colored" school on Merry Green Hill, which "went through the eighth grade." It was a short and pleasant walk from his home through fragrant fields, and the teacher was not a hard taskmaster. "But when I was seven," he was to write later, "I began to get into trouble. It happened this way. In spelling, if the word was dog, stove, dishpan, or something like that, I had a sketch of the article at the end of the word. And the results were, I would have to stay in after school and finish my lesson the right way. This happened frequently and I just couldn't help it. The worst part of it was, I would get a beating when I got home, for coming home late, regardless of what I was kept in for."

Every Sunday the Pippins would walk down the dirt road and cross the railroad tracks to East Main Street and the Goshen Methodist Church. East Main Street was a broad and beautiful thoroughfare, with a green between its dusty lanes and street lamps to brighten its evenings.

Beyond the church was the historic Orange Inn, a landmark since 1790, and beyond that the homes of the rich—colonial stone and brick mansions, set back on rolling green lawns, some with great two-story windows, and others with Victorian "gingerbread." General Grant himself had stayed in one of these homes, and watched the Goshen trotting races from its barn.

The church was a dark Victorian-Gothic affair of red brick and pointed arches. Inside, its semi-circular pews faced the altar like an amphitheater. The ceiling of dark green vaulting might have been forbidding had it not received light from a rose window of stained glass.

As he came out of church, Horace would look across the street to the yellow county courthouse, with its white Doric columns and Corinthian lantern. Goshen had been the county seat since 1737 and its courthouse, constructed in 1843, was the cause of considerable civic pride.

Across Main Street was the tall shaft of the Revolutionary War monument, erected to the memory of those twenty men of Goshen who died in the Battle of Minisink, July 22, 1779. "They Still Live," the inscription asserted. Just up the block, beside the Orange Inn, was Barney Clark's restaurant, where for a nickel a boy could buy an ice cream soda or a glass of Barney's specialty, "Mountain Dew."

Peeking through the buildings, directly across Main Street, was the Goshen Race Track. Goshen had always been a center for horses, and when back in 1781, racing on Main Street became a bit dangerous, a track had been laid out on the nearby field. It had been improved year after year, and finally in 1874 a large oval track had been constructed and a grandstand built. The wealthy railroad magnate E. H. Harriman was soon to acquire the major interest in the track and to promote its reputation so that he later had to finance a luxury hotel for the crowds it attracted. Goshen was the home of the trotting thoroughbreds, the most beautiful horses in the world; the home of Imported Messenger, the great-granddaddy of them all, and of the nation's most important trotting race, the Hambletonian.

Horace would wander about the stables, marveling at the beauty of the animals, stroking their noses, and then —with pencil and paper—trying to capture some of that loveliness.

His passion to draw was hampered only by a lack of materials, and that was a problem he tried constantly to solve. "One day," he wrote, "I got a magazine with a lot of advertisements in it of dry goods. In this magazine there was a sketch of a very funny face. Under this face printed in large letters it said make me and win a prize. And I did and sent it to Chicago, to the address that was given. The following week the prize came. It was a box of crayon pencils of six different colors. Also a box of cold water paint and two brushes. These I delighted in and used them often."

Like most of his people, Horace spent the better part of his indoor life in the kitchen. In many black homes the kitchen was the only room. DOMINO PLAYERS (Color-plate 4) and SUNDAY MORNING BREAKFAST are the strongest of the many pictures he was to paint years later out of these memories.

DOMINO PLAYERS is a masterpiece of patterning in subdued colors with the dominoes themselves a bridge between the red cap, the polka-dotted blouse and the intricate reds of the needlework leading into the fiery teeth of the kitchen grate.

In SUNDAY MORNING BREAKFAST there is a similar
give-and-take between the grate and the wife's checker-
board apron, but the mood is more somber. The very
emptiness of the room sets off the broken chair, the slats
showing through the walls where the plaster has fallen
off, and the husband putting on his shoes as he looks
sidewise with a baleful frown at the bowl of porridge
the children are receiving.

Horace was always looking for an opportunity to use
his paints, so he was delighted when an opportunity arose
to donate some work to a Sunday school festival.
From a yard of muslin, he cut six doilies, fringing their
edges and leaving the centers for his pictures. With his
colored pencils he carefully drew six biblical scenes—
Jesus Ascending in the Chariot of Fire, Daniel in the
Lion's Den, Moses in the Fiery Bush, the Beggar at the
Gate, etc.

At the church, the woman hung them on a wire to
be sold and gently shooed all the children into the
church yard to play. Later, when Horace came in for
his refreshments, he discovered that the doilies had been
sold and rushed to share the good news with his mother.

Several days later on his way to school he was stopped
by an old woman who asked if he wasn't Horace Pippin. When he said that he was, she drew out of her
apron a clean fringed doily, devoid of any picture. "You
certainly make some bum things," she said. "I bought
this at the festival with a picture on it. I washed it and
this is all I have."

It must have been at that moment that Horace first

THE MILKMAN OF GOSHEN (1945) Owned by Ruth Gordon

realized the need for a more stable medium—for an art that would last.

Horace painted only one picture of the New York town where he had spent his childhood. It is a good picture, but not a particularly revealing one. It does show that his memories of that time were happy. THE MILKMAN OF GOSHEN depicts a delivery wagon drawn by a white horse, standing in front of a two-story frame house—quite possibly the Pippin house at 339 West Main Street—while two women with shawls around their shoulders wait to receive the milk from the big cans. A little black girl, no higher than the wheel she stands beside, waves to the milkman. It is an autumn day. Pods and bright leaves are falling from a tree in the yard, making a gay pattern on the road; and an opened tin can on the near side may be there to indicate the orderly artist's disapproval of litter-bugs.

On October 26, 1898, the Goshen records show that Daniel W. Pippin, a black laborer, died at the age of twenty-six. This may well have been Horace's father, for in that same year Christine Pippin went to the country to work at a hotel, and the following year to Middletown to work for a private family.

Middletown was only a ten-cent trolley ride from Goshen, and halfway between the two towns was Midway Park. On hot summer evenings residents of both towns would meet at the park, ride the roller coaster and the merry-go-round, and watch the exciting balloon ascensions of Maggie Dailey of Middletown. There were penny arcades, nickelodeons, band concerts, boating, bathing, dancing, and picnics. Not the least of the fun was the trolley itself, whose open carriages swayed through the countryside past the Wallkill River while the beribboned ladies held onto their enormous hats.

Perhaps it was on one such excursion that Christine Pippin, Horace's mother, met a man named Green, whom she married shortly afterward. The Greens were soon to produce for Horace four sisters: Nan, Hattie, Mary, and Sally.

All of the children would listen not only to Christine's patient Bible readings, but to the tales she would tell of the past, and most especially to the one tale handed down to her from her mother, the tale of John Brown.

Brown, a fanatical white abolitionist, had staged his armed attack on the arsenal at Harpers Ferry, Virginia, on October 16, 1859, and Christine Pippin's mother had watched his hanging at nearby Charlestown December 2 of that fateful year.

Years later Horace would paint three of his best pictures about this legendary hero of his childhood. The first and greatest of them, JOHN BROWN GOING TO HIS HANGING (Colorplate 1) shows exactly the scene his mother so often described.

The procession is passing the white farmhouses set against the Blue Ridge Mountains. It is the view which led the historical John Brown to remark, "This *is* beautiful country. I never had the pleasure of seeing it before!" How accurately Horace's grandmother must have remembered the occasion is shown by the authenticity of every detail in the painting: the almost leafless December trees, the spectators along the route with scarves around their necks and hands in pockets, the barred window (the jail?) in the background, and Brown himself with his arms bound to his sides riding his own coffin on a wagon drawn by a pair of white horses. Some of the Southern whites watch curiously, and some chat together indifferently as people do when they are not involved in a tragedy. But the dominant figure in the picture is the single black slave—Horace's grandmother very likely—who turns away from the procession to confront the viewer with an expression at once fearless and accusing.

How much of his grandmother's memory is contained in the other two pictures of John Brown that Horace was to paint it is hard to say, but there is the same authenticity of detail and mood.

The second picture depicts the trial. The bearded Brown, still suffering from the wounds he received at Harpers Ferry, did indeed lie on a stretcher at the foot of his twelve bearded jurymen (Brown's Southern counsel-for-the-defense did not challenge any one of them). And Brown did indeed carry his documents—his maps, his Constitution, his "Vindication of the Invasion," and his letters from Frederick Douglass and other Northern Abolitionists—in a flowered carpetbag. (There is one such still lying in the basement of the Chester County Historical Society's Museum, which Horace haunted at the time he was painting these pictures, and which he no doubt copied.)

The third picture, JOHN BROWN READING HIS BIBLE, carries more emotional weight than the other two. Perhaps this is because it is so lacking in action, so bare and quiet, yet filled with such a foreboding tension. Again, the scene is authentic. Brown had started life as a free-thinker but soon returned to the Calvinist faith of his father, reading his Bible, his biographers say, "with

JOHN BROWN READING HIS BIBLE (1942) Courtesy of the
Makler Gallery, Philadelphia

singleminded determination." His speeches were filled
with quotations from Scripture and he used to delight
in correcting those who misquoted. This was the Brown
that Horace painted in a log cabin resembling a jail cell,

30

reading at night by candlelight. This was the Brown who memorized the doomsday prophecies of Isaiah and Jeremiah—"And I will feed them that oppress thee with their own flesh; and they shall be drunken with their own blood, as with sweet wine"—Brown the accuser, implacable, unforgiving.

Horace didn't have much time to listen to these exciting stories, for soon he was whisked off to work. Mr. Green, shortly after fathering the daughters, seems to have disappeared from the scene, and Horace, the oldest child, was hired out to earn bread for the family.

At fourteen, he found himself on the farm of Mr. James Gavin, who was to recognize his talent and offer to send him to art school. However, when his mother became ill, Horace returned to Goshen and went to work in a coalyard, a feed store, and from job to job. Finally, hearing that a porter was wanted at the St. Elmo Hotel, he hastened to apply. The St. Elmo had a legendary proprietor, and Horace's friends warned that he wouldn't work for that man three weeks. Horace took the job anyway. He stayed seven years.

The St. Elmo was owned by "Boss" Hock, a man so demanding and so powerful that many would have feared to serve him for even "three weeks." Robert B. Hock built the 52-room St. Elmo in 1887 across the narrow street from the Erie depot. Salesmen and politicians, newspapermen and judges stayed in its rooms before it burned to the ground in 1920.

In its famous "Amen Corner," politicians were made and broken. After Hock was appointed County Clerk in 1881, he was the recognized Republican "boss" of

Orange County, but Democrats as well as Republicans planned their campaigns under his roof and sought his aid. It was said that even Governor Odell was forced to seek peace with Hock in order to survive. Heated debates took place at the St. Elmo, but when Hock ended them with his "Amen!" the decision was final.

In the big chairs that lined its porches, the townsfolk gossiped and took their siestas. The courthouse brought judges and lawyers to town. Murder trials, like that in which Burton Gibson was accused of drowning Countess Rose Szabo in Greenwood Lake, brought out the national press. Racing, horse shows, and boxing matches which were held in Goshen's Brownleigh Park, brought noted sports writers, and the "racing crowd." All stayed at the St. Elmo.

Hock had his lighter side. The town children called him "Pa," for he was like a father to hundreds of them, and would pay them nicely for the contribution of a live bullfrog to feed to the alligators he kept in the cellar. In 1900 when Hock was mayor of Goshen he had come up with the idea of importing alligators from Florida to enliven the ponds in Church Park, and so he did. The animals were evidently fairly docile in summer for the records do not mention anyone being devoured by them. But in winter they were a problem. They could not live outdoors in Goshen's cold climate. At first the crafty mayor got the Minisink Fire Department to board his beasts, but when the firemen objected he provided them with tanks at the St. Elmo.

Horace, under Hock's roof, met a wide variety of people, but he had to work hard, finding little time to sketch their faces and clothing. Still, he often overheard their stories. He remembered especially General Grant's visit to Goshen, and the talk of Grant's commander, whose kind, forgiving nature was more to his liking than John Brown's inflexible one.

Horace would paint many pictures of this man later on. First he would show the young Abe Lincoln and his father building their log cabin at Pigeon Creek. A second painting showed Lincoln as THE GOOD SAMARITAN. But Horace's major picture of the wartime President was the one painted in the year of the John Brown trilogy: Lincoln in his tent, flanked by a skeptical General Grant and two ramrod infantrymen standing at attention with raised bayonets, pardoning the soldier who had gone to sleep on sentry duty. Lincoln, the kindly Emancipator.

In 1911 Horace's mother died, and he wasted no time in leaving both the St. Elmo and Goshen. He went first to Paterson, New Jersey, where he worked for the Fidelity Storage House on its moving vans. His job was to pack furniture for shipment all over the United States, and he always asked for the assignment of crating pictures. For a few moments he would run his fingers over the rough canvases, noting the thickness of the paint or the fine lines with which the artist had drawn details. It was the closest Horace had ever gotten to a museum.

In 1916 he heard of an opportunity to become a molder, leaving his job for one at the American Brakeshoe Company in Mahwah up the Ramapo. He had been there only a few months when the United States became involved in World War I.

"The good old U.S.A.," Horace wrote in his war diary, "was in trouble with Germany and to do our duty to her we had to leave here." Like most Americans in 1917, Horace was eager to "do his duty" and to "make the world safe for democracy" as President Wilson put it so hopefully. Most black Americans felt that if the United States won, and they had a hand in the victory, their lives would be better and safer. The democracy they were helping to save would in turn save them.

"In March 1917 I gave two weeks notice to quit," he writes. "On my last day I was called to the head office and the superintendent said to me, you have your applications in for winding up today, haven't you? I said, yes, Sir! And you are going into the Army, aren't you? I said yes, I am going with the fifteenth New York regiment. He said if you come back your job will be waiting for you and I wish you good luck and God's speed."

Between July and December of 1917 Horace was stationed at Fort Dix, New Jersey, and Camp Wadsworth, South Carolina. Then, from the time he landed at Brest, France, on December 27, 1917, until Christmas Day of the following year, when he was evacuated on a hospital ship, there followed a year of his life—the only year—which he has written about in detail.

This account he laboriously wrote in capitals, in longhand, and in dictated typescript no fewer than four times. There is no hint in any of the manuscripts that Horace was horrified by war, resented his role in this particular one, or ever felt a twinge of guilt or self-pity. On the contrary a note of exhilaration runs through the narratives. He was simply doing his duty as a citizen, unpleasant, boring, and dangerous as the job might occasionally be. He took the kind of pride in his outfit a professional ballplayer does in his team. The enemy— was the enemy. Soldiering was one of life's burdens, but no more so than being poor or doing backbreaking manual labor. No inquiry into the causes. No concern for the results. If one survived, one was lucky. At the very least one owed gratitude to God.

Horace's desire to join the armed forces was not an isolated case. Throughout the country—North and South—black men no less than whites were clamoring to join up. And the Army, far from organized for the task at hand, was quite uncertain about what to do with blacks.

Segregation had been the rule ever since the Civil War, and mixing the two races was never even considered. It was believed that white soldiers would riot if asked to march shoulder to shoulder with black men. Should there then be whole black regiments and divisions? The specter of a division of black men sent fear into the hearts of many whites. Consequently, while the Army agreed to black regiments, it was careful not to form an entire black division.

Most of the black recruits, it was decided, would be used as common laborers, to haul the equipment, build the roads and trenches, dig the graves. They would not be given training in the use of firearms. Of the 100,000 black men who were sent to France, 80,000 were part of the Service of Supplies (SOS). Nor were there any plans to train black officers for these regiments, though pressure finally forced the Army to train a few.

The black regiment which Horace hurried to join was the New York State 15th National Guard. It was organized by Charles W. Fillmore, a black New Yorker who became a captain in it, but it had primarily white officers, most of them from prominent New York families. Its white commander, Colonel William Hayward, was exceptional. He appreciated his black fighters. "I wish I had a brigade, a division, or a corps of them," he was to write some months later. "We'd make history."

Upon its acceptance into the United States Army, the 15th National Guard was rechristened the 369th Infantry Regiment, but it was still known to its members as the "Old Fifteenth." After a few weeks of drill at Fort Dix and a few months guard duty there and elsewhere, the regiment was sent to Camp Wadsworth in Spartanburg, South Carolina.

The mayor of this southern city greeted the regiment with suspicion. "With their Northern ideas about race equality," he warned, "they will probably expect to be treated like white men." But the men of the 369th did their best to win southern friends. They had within their ranks two talented jazz musicians, Lieutenant James Reece Europe and Drum Major Noble Sissle. Europe and Sissle had long since organized a regimental band, and they now offered to have the band perform for the townspeople.

About ten days after the arrival of the regiment, and after two concerts had been held, Sissle went into a hotel to see if he could buy a New York newspaper. The hotel manager attacked him and knocked him down. Sissle, who had been warned to avoid trouble, picked up his hat to leave. However several white soldiers from New York, incensed by the unprovoked assault, rushed the hotel manager and would have beaten him had not Sissle and Europe calmed them down.

There had been several earlier incidents, and this latest trouble made the divisional commander and the Army

Chief of Staff nervous. They ordered the 369th out of Spartanburg at once. So, less than two weeks after it had arrived, the 369th, without having received the training intended for it, was sent back to New York, there to become the first black unit shipped abroad.

Horace's war diaries make no mention of these incidents, but his account does indicate that the Navy was as unprepared to cope with the 369th as the Army had been. In fact, the regiment's departure from New York, in his account, bears less resemblance to an efficient wartime operation than to a Marx Brothers movie.

The ship *Pocahontas* was to make three false starts before finally getting under way for France. On the first try, something went wrong with the driving bar and, after a day at sea, the ship had to be returned to New York for repairs. The 369th was sent to the Armory at 133rd Street, where they waited. A month passed.

The second time out, fire was discovered in the coal bin and again the regiment was put ashore.

On December 3 they went aboard again in a howling blizzard. The boat lay in the harbor overnight and at midnight another ship, the *Hawk*, struck it on the port side. The hole it gouged was, luckily, above the water line, and the crew worked all night cementing it up. At dawn, the ship left on schedule, and this time managed to cross the Atlantic, arriving at Brest on December 27.

There, the regiment was packed standing up, into boxcars, headed for St. Nazaire. For two days and two nights, without room to sit down and growing stiff with the cold, the soldiers jolted against each other as the train moved on.

France in the winter of 1918 was a cold, grim place. Caught in the throes of heavy snows and icy weather, its army bases were not equipped for the sudden influx of hundreds of thousands of American soldiers. The accommodations were crude and the work was hard.

Between December and February the 369th laid over five hundred miles of railroad track inland from the sea. Later when the United States was to send heavy cargo, munitions, and supplies, it would travel over these tracks on its journey to the front.

There was little rest. "We went to bed in the dark and got up in the dark," Horace writes, "only the moon showing. . . . Sometimes we drilled eight hours a day, and were good, good enough to go any place."

But the 369th was kept on labor detail. When would they be given a chance to *fight?* Horace must have wondered. The desire of the typical American soldier in World War I was to get into the trenches, to deal the Germans a personal, lethal blow. And no doubt this feeling was heightened in black regiments, left behind to "do the dirty work" while white ones went forward to win glory.

Undoubtedly they would have been kept on labor detail until the end of the war—making Horace's war remembrances and subsequent life substantially different —if the Germans had not launched an offensive on March 21, 1918. The French and British armies were in danger of being crushed. General "Black Jack" Pershing needed every available American to save the situation. But though he would have preferred to lead the American Expeditionary Force into battle as a unit, not enough Americans had yet arrived, and the Allied armies must be saved. Therefore the American soldiers in France had to be attached to the French or British armies. The British made it clear that they did not care to take on the 369th, but the French, who for three years had been fighting side by side with their own black colonial troops had no such objection. Accordingly, the 369th was attached to the French 16th Division and sent into brief combat training with them. The French were "delighted with them," Colonel Hayward wrote, "and taught them everything they knew. The French soldiers have not the slightest prejudice," he continued, "and we have all become great chums who eat, dance, sing, march and fight together in absolute accord."

"We were formally transferred to the French High Command," Horace writes. "After a month's training learning the French rifle, the 369th was sent into action . . . We took to them lonely, cooty, muddy trenches."

Horace's very first paintings were to come out of the vivid memory of what followed, but he waited until the last year of his life to sum up what he had just gone through. He must have put THE BARRACKS off so long because he sensed that it would require his full powers to describe inaction without painting a vacuum, boredom without being boring about it. The scene could double for the trenches. Four soldiers under-

THE BARRACKS (1945) Courtesy of The Phillips Collection, Washington

ground in their improvised bunks are doing their thing —sleeping, mending clothes, writing letters—as isolated one from another as though in solitary confinement.

As always with great painters, the message is conveyed by pictorial means. In this case the horizontals and verticals from which there is no escape; the depressing gradations of grays and browns suggesting death; the murky candlelight providing just enough illumination of such significant details as the black hand on the white pad, the guns and gas masks, the muddy floor.

For this picture which meant so much to him, Horace did something he had never done before. He painted a small preliminary sketch, twelve inches by nine. It is brilliantly painted but lacks many of the master strokes of the big painting: the outlining of the hand against the letter, the disquieting shadows of the seated soldiers, the patches of olive drab on the upright posts. Most important, he left out the floor, receding from lavender to black shadow under the lower bunks, thus greatly increasing the feeling of loneliness. What the final canvas perfectly conveys is the sense of man's utter isolation in war, trapped like an animal, polishing equipment, sleeping like the dead, living in loud boredom, always "together" but never for an instant truly alone.

"All we could hear was the shells," Horace writes. "They would burst all the time. I got so used to them that I did not mind them at all."

In May the Germans launched the major attack of their final offensive. In three days they crossed the Marne and pushed to within thirty-seven miles of Paris. The word went out to all the Allied troops: Hold the line! Do not let them pass!

From April until early July the 369th was under constant fire as one of the units stationed just to the west of the Argonne Forest. During that time, and throughout the war, it never lost a prisoner, a trench, or a foot of ground.

"They are positively the most stoical and mysterious men I've ever known," Colonel Hayward was to write about his men. "Nothing surprises them. The French say they are entirely different from their own African troops and the Indian troops of the British, who are so exciteable under shellfire. Of course, I have explained that my boys are public school boys, wise in their day and generation, accustomed to the terrible noises of the subway, elevated and street traffic of New York City (which would drive any desert man or Himalayan mountaineer mad) and are all Christians. . . . They know the damned child-killing Germans are firing at them with pyrocellulose [gas] and they know how the breech mechanism works."

Part of the time the 369th was in charge of more than a mile of the front. Each night the regiment would send out small patrols to attack the German trenches, get information, and take prisoners. The Germans likewise would send their soldiers across "No Man's Land" to probe the Allied lines.

On the night of May 13, 1918, a twenty-four-man German patrol stealthily made its way into the area held by the 369th, and attacked a post held by Private Needham Roberts and Private Henry Johnson. Johnson sent up a rocket for help, and then both men, though wounded, proceeded to lob grenades at the enemy. Johnson, after firing all three cartridges in his rifle, crashed it on the head of an enemy soldier, knocking him out. Finally, before being cut down by pistol shots, he killed two more Germans with his knife and dispersed those who followed with his remaining grenades.

When help arrived, both men had been badly wounded. Captain Little feared for their lives. "Captain, sir," said Johnson, "you don't have to worry about me. I've been shot before." But to everyone's delight, both men lived and were awarded the Croix de Guerre, the highest French decoration, for their heroism. Since they were the first black Americans to receive this honor, the 369th was suddenly famous. Colonel Hayward, however, reserved his greatest praise for the teamwork of the regiment. "If I ask for twelve volunteers," he wrote, "the whole company falls in and I have to promise assignments days in advance."

"Some time in July," Horace writes, "one of the strangest things happened. We were planning to go on a raid. They didn't force anyone to go. It was all voluntary. The zero hour had been posted at twelve o'clock. At 11:30 we were at the P.C. getting our final instructions. While we were there a boy in the outfit . . . looked like every nerve was shaking. I never saw a man like this before. I asked him what was wrong. His eyes all but bulged out of his head, he said he was not coming back. I told him that he didn't have to go into this raid. He volunteered himself. And if you are sick you can be exempted, but he said no I am going through with it but I am not coming back.

"We left the P.C. quarter to twelve. It was the worst fifteen minutes I ever put in, watching this boy. We were on our way to our starting point. We arrived in our places about one minute before the artillery began to fire. As soon as they did we jumped over the top for the enemy trenches. Five minutes later we were back in our trenches again with two German prisoners. And the boy didn't come back, as he said. A German had run him through. He foretold his end. I often think of him in this respect. I have seen men die in all forms and shapes but never one who knew like he did."

Danger, suffering, and sudden death were everyday occurrences for the 369th. At one time the regiment was under fire for *one hundred and thirty days without relief*—an incredible endurance record. One of the reasons they were kept in the front lines was that no provisions had been made at the rear for recreation zones for blacks. Segregation was strictly enforced, though few of the soldiers were aware of it; nor were they permitted days of leave in French cities. Their only recreation, in fact, came from the shows which their own regimental band put on for them.

During these days and months in the trenches Horace was constantly writing in his diary and making sketches. He was fascinated with both the factual horrors of war and the beauty of the French countryside. But as he moved forward from battle to battle most of these drawings had to be discarded and were lost forever.

Fortunately one series of sketches escaped this fate, six drawings that illustrate one of the diaries. They are the earliest surviving work from the artist's hand.

The first sketch illustrates a grueling forced march (". . . but we kept on and on"). Three doughboys

in full battle gear slouch along by a section of board
fence. The heaviness of their appearance is impressive,
and so are the nails in the fence so important to the
design.

The second (". . . and this is one of the places that
the Germans gave us plenty of gas") is a landscape of
brown, intricately woven tree limbs against a pale blue
sky. The foreground is divided between grass and some
sort of metal casement studded with rivets.

The third illustrates a second gas attack. Two masked figures are in a trench. Barbed wire against a green field provides the patterning this time.

WAR DIARY SKETCHES From the Book *Horace Pippin, A Negro Painter in America*, by Selden Rodman. Copyright 1947 by The Quadrangle Press, Inc. Reprinted by permission of Selden Rodman.

The fourth illustrates the following sentence: ". . . As he got up over the strip of cedar, he open up on the German plane, and all at once she were afire and come down to rise no more." The cedars are delicately massed in pencil to one side. The Allied aircraft, blue-red-white circles on its wings and spurting flame through its prop, is pointing at the enemy plane, a fiery wreck across from the cedars.

The fifth is the most complex. The foreground is divided into two graceful slopes, a black fortification nestling between them. Three soldiers with bayonets poised are moving up one slope between bomb-bursts like evil flowers. "We kept on going, the shells were bursting fast as we made the hill . . ."

The sixth and simplest is entirely in pencil. ("We could not travel without being seen by the skyline . . .") Night is scratched above and below the tell-tale seam of light through which the soldiers crawl like miners in a vein of coal.

Early in September the 369th was transferred from the 16th French Division and made an integral part of the 161st French Division. Rumors were going around that there was going to be a big drive. The Allies were preparing their biggest offensive. Instead of "Hold the line!" the order was about to be "Attack!" The 369th, the "Hell-Fighters" as they were now called by both the French and Germans, were to be in the thick of it from start to finish. On September 26 they went "over the top" and took the town of Séchault. They remained in the front lines until mid-October, when they became the first Allied unit to reach the Rhine.

1 JOHN BROWN GOING TO HIS HANGING (1942) Courtesy of
the Philadelphia Academy of the Fine Arts

2   END OF THE WAR: STARTING HOME (1931) Courtesy of
the Philadelphia Museum of Art: Given by Robert Carlen

3 WEST CHESTER COURT HOUSE (1940) Owned by Mr. and Mrs. David J. Grossman. Photograph courtesy of *The Philadelphia Inquirer*

4   Domino Players (1943) Courtesy of The Phillips Collection, Washington

5   Amish Letter Writer (1940) Owned by Mr. and Mrs. Samuel L. Feldman. Photograph courtesy of *The Philadelphia Inquirer*

6 VICTORIAN INTERIOR (1946) Courtesy of the Metropolitan
Museum of Art: Arthur H. Hearn Fund, 1958

7   THE HOLY MOUNTAIN III (1945) Lent by the Joseph H.
Hirshhorn Collection

8 MAN ON A BENCH (1946) From the collection of Mrs.
Sidney E. Cohn

"The time had come when we were to give up everything we had," Horace writes, "extra shirts, pants and shoes. We only had two blankets, tooth brush and tooth paste as we started for the Champagne sector that morning . . . The artillery was lined along the road as far as you could see, hub to hub, all kinds and makes . . . When they opened up you would have thought the world was coming to an end . . . To see those shells bursting was a pretty sight. But the gas, dust and smoke was terrible . . . By night we laid along the crest of a hill where the enemy machine gun fire was so great we had to change our position and get to a flank to get over that hill. Men laying all over, wounded and dead. Some was being carried. We wished we could help the wounded but we couldn't. We had to leave them there and keep advancing, ducking from shell hole to shell hole all day. That night I counted fourteen machine gun nests out of order in our path . . .

"Next morning came like the rest but the machine gun fire wasn't as heavy . . . The snipers were plentiful and I remember spotting a shell hole and making a run for it. Just as I was within three feet and getting ready to dive in I was hit in the shoulder. There was four in that shell hole. One bound my wound the best he could and they all left me alone. I thought I could crawl out and get to a first aid station, but a sniper kept me in the hole so long I lost too much blood to get out on my own power.

"It was late in the afternoon when the French snipers came by. One stopped at the shell hole where I was shot and I beckoned to him to get down and tried to explain that the sniper was there and would get him. While I was trying to explain to him, a bullet passed through his head and it didn't even knock his helmet off. He stood there for at least ten seconds before he slipped down, and when he did he slid down on top of me. I had lost so much blood by this time I couldn't even move him.

"After a while a French sergeant came by and was surprised to see his buddy dead. I motioned to him to get down and he did. He sat in the shell hole with me and he told another man to get the sniper. A minute after that I heard the French rifle and knew the sniper wasn't there any more. He came back, said that he got him.

"Two stretcher bearers came by and got me out of the hole and laid me on the path. It started to rain that morning about nine and it rained all day and at night it increased. My stretcher was full of water. About ten o'clock that night reinforcements were coming up. I could hear them splashing in the mud. Some nearly stepped upon me. Finally the reinforcement had taken over this sector and sent their stretcher bearers after me.

"I was taken to a dugout. The doctor looked my wound over and I went to sleep. The next morning I woke up and dead men were on both sides of me. They were carrying the wounded out and leaving the dead in the dugout. It was still raining. It wasn't long before a French officer came along with German prisoners and they carried me down to the road where the ambulance could pick us up . . ."

Horace was taken to a field hospital at Léon, where an operation was performed on his wounded shoulder. A few days later he was sent to Vichy to the Hotel St. de Baine, which was being used as a hospital.

By Christmas the wound had healed and he was transferred to Brest, where a hospital ship, the *Northern Pacific*, waited to carry him home.

Arriving in New York on January 5, 1919, he was sent first to the Far Hill Hospital at Long Beach, Long Island, and later to Fort Ontario on Lake Ontario.

According to Horace's obituary in the New York *Times*, he was immediately awarded the French Croix de Guerre. But twenty-seven years passed before the American Army got around to presenting its lowest combat decoration, the Purple Heart, which is given automatically to any soldier wounded in battle. That notification came to him on September 13, 1945, when Horace Pippin was already a famous man.

"I was discharged May 22nd, 1919," Horace writes. "My right arm was bound to me. I could not use it for anything. But my mind runs back to the sketches I had made in France which I had to destroy."

THE END OF THE WAR: STARTING HOME (Colorplate 2), which Horace was to paint some ten years later in the memory of those sketches, was no triumphant march, no happy homecoming. The sky is full of flaming planes and ugly shellbursts. The mountain is a scrap heap. The trees glisten menacingly. The earth is pierced with cruel stakes, and between the tangles of wire the opposing soldiers, as though too far gone to respond to the news normally, come out of their holes in the earth to confront each other, their faces without expression, like corpses on Judgment Day.

No other picture that he painted afterward is so loaded with paint, so crowded with figures and objects and events, so full of a sense of tortured earth and violent movement. And that this crowding is deliberate may be seen from the frame itself, which the artist himself decorated with heavy wood carvings of all the deadly weapons.

Two other paintings by Horace Pippin add to a cycle of modern war scenes that no other artist has approached in power.

GAS ALARM OUTPOSTS: ARGONNE SECTOR, painted in 1931, shows three soldiers standing as though stunned before a screen of wire nicely camouflaged with autumn leaves. A few clouds and observation balloons fail to fill the sky. But the startling feature of this picture is a section of railroad tracks, remembered no doubt from those early days in France when so many miles had been laid. The tracks rise from the foreground until chopped off abruptly by the wire. The effect is enhanced by disregard of perspective so that the tracks seem to writhe upward and then vanish.

They supply the same note as the footsteps in SHELL HOLES AND OBSERVATION BALLOON, painted the same year. The footprints have no beginning and no end. Entering from the right of the picture, they pass the shattered buildings in the background and the two gigantic sinister craters in the left foreground, behind which the distant balloon (the only sign of "life" in the canvas) ominously rises. The color is very scant: olive-

SHELL HOLES AND OBSERVATION BALLOON: CHAMPAGNE SEC-
TOR (1931) Lent by The Baltimore Museum of Art

green grass and roofs, gray roads, craters and sky, glaring
whitewashed farmhouses with black fissures. No more.

This dark technique was an effective means of con-
veying that aloneness—man the hunter and man the
hunted—that all Horace Pippin's early paintings were to

53

THE GET-AWAY (1939) Bequest of Miss Ellen Winsor and
Mrs. Edmund Evans to Bryn Mawr College. Photograph lent
by The Carlen Galleries, Inc., Philadelphia

convey. It doesn't matter that in THE GET-AWAY it is
a fox that is being hunted. The isolation of the animal
caught against the whiteness of the snow is like that
of the soldier. The moonlight reflected off those olive-
golden clouds has the same effect as the star shells in
No Man's Land. There is no way out.

The paintings and the notebook drawings reveal at
once what the diary conceals. The war had been a

shattering experience to Horace Pippin. He would not have admitted it. He may not even have "known" it. But the drawings, and to a far greater degree the war paintings that grew out of them, are evidence that cannot be denied. He had seen the desolation of earth, the ruin of cities, the inhumanity of man. The Bible said that all men were brothers, and Horace believed this as firmly as he believed anything. Then what was the meaning of this Thing they had sent him into, this suffering and this killing? He could not say. There could be only one way to get at the truth. But his right arm, the only instrument he had to let out what was fighting inside him, had been paralyzed by a sniper's bullet.

When Horace Pippin came home from the war, he was at loose ends. He could not go back to the job that was waiting for him in Mahwah, New Jersey. He doubted that he could work at any job. His right arm, fastened to his shoulder by a steel plate, hung at his side like a dead thing.

His army disability pension of $22.50 a month would hardly provide for his needs. Where should he go? What should he do? Horace was uncertain.

He went briefly to visit his brother, John, in Belleville, New Jersey, where a friend, hearing of his plight, hurried to introduce him to Ora Jennie Featherstone Wade. Ora Jennie, who was four years older than Horace, had been twice married, twice widowed, and had a six-year-old son to support. "She needed a man," the friend reasoned, "and Pip needed a woman." The army pension, while not large, was nevertheless a dependable income, not subject to the vagaries of unemployment. It would help to support Ora Jennie and her son; and she, in turn, would care for Pippin, seeing to all his needs and comforts. On November 21, 1920, they were married.

Ora Jennie was a short, stocky woman, five feet high and weighing over two hundred pounds. She wore horn-rimmed glasses and was fond of print dresses. She was quiet, kind, tender-hearted, and her feelings were easily hurt.

She saw in Pippin a handsome man, over six feet tall and powerfully built, with an open expressive face, and one crippled arm. Even then he had the courtly manners of an old-fashioned aristocrat and wore dark suits with vests—which, because of his height, never quite reached his trousers. The sleeves of his white shirts were habitually ringed with flowered elastics, to keep the cuffs from slipping down and getting soiled.

Ora Jennie had been born in Greensboro, North Carolina, and had worked in Hudson, New York. But now she lived, as did most of the Featherstones, in West Chester, Pennsylvania. And so by strange coincidence it was to West Chester, a town which Pippin could not remember but where, nevertheless, he had been born, that he now returned.

The Pippins moved into the narrow brick house at 327 West Gay Street. Just up the hill Gay Street became West Chester's "Main Street," but here across the tracks trees shaded the rough brick sidewalks and children played in the stillness.

The house had four rooms on the ground floor and three on each of the two upper levels—plenty of space for Horace and Ora Jennie and seven-year-old Richard

Wade. "We rattled around that house," Wade was later to recall.

Ora Jennie took in laundry to supplement their income and Pippin helped to deliver it. She was a good house-keeper and an excellent cook and took special pride in the flowers she grew in their small back yard. Horace liked to sit there watching the buds come to blossom and the strut of his magnificently plumed roosters and chickens. Sometimes he would wrestle with the neighborhood children and photograph them when they played at "dressing up."

The painting he made of the block of Gay Street houses is now in the Wichita (Kansas) Art Museum. It contrasts very beautifully the rows of brick, patched here and there where windows and a chimney must have been inserted as afterthoughts, with a lordly catalpa tree in full bloom.

West Chester was a small, sociable town, one mile square, where most of the 11,717 inhabitants knew one another. Like Goshen it was a county seat, and consequently distinguished by an imposing courthouse and a considerable amount of local prestige. On North High Street the wealthy whites lived side by side, "on their accumulated incomes" as a townsman put it. Handsome brick and stone mansions with tall, many-paned windows were flanked by spacious lawns, shade trees, and gardens.

There were many beautiful buildings in West Chester, but the County Court House was not one of them. Perhaps that was why Pippin painted it (Colorplate 3). It was a challenge. And anyone who has seen the picture knows how well that challenge was met. The trees are a little greener, the clouds a little rounder, the sky a little bluer, the bricks a little brickier. The war memorial, a tired bronze soldier burdened with an enormous flag, points to the clock tower with a knowing air, as if to say, "Time to go back to civilian life." The Stars and Stripes on a staff above the gable join the party, giving birth to eight flaglets on the lawn below. The window shades turn yellow. A schoolboy prepares to throw his books in the air. Even the lowly fireplug becomes a swinger, putting on a bright red cap and throwing out its stubby arms as if to embrace the first dog that sidles by.

Pippin passed that courthouse day after day as he delivered the laundry or walked young Richard to school. As in Goshen, the schools were segregated, and the boy had to go clear across town to the "colored" school, returning home for lunch, and then making the long trek back and forth again.

But while the schools were segregated, many local organizations were not, and in such a one as the American Legion, blacks and whites met unself-consciously. Pippin, an ardent Legionnaire, just as he had been an ardent soldier, organized the Legion's drum and bugle corps and led it in parades throughout the county. Ora Jennie was a diligent worker for the Legion Auxiliary, and they would dress in their Legion uniforms and go to meetings as far away as Harrisburg. "Pip came along to the county meetings about 80 per cent of the time," Legionnaire Ed Valentine remembers. "He was a jolly fellow and liked to joke about how he got that wound in France."

PIPPIN AND HIS FAMILY From the book *Horace Pippin, A Negro Painter in America*, by Selden Rodman. Copyright 1947 by The Quadrangle Press, Inc. Reprinted by permission of Selden Rodman.

The Pippins were believing Christians, reading the Bible at home as well as attending service on Sundays. In their early wedded years they went to the Methodist Church, then briefly to Faith Tabernacle, a "healing church" where Horace sought some relief from the pain of his wound. In their last years they were Baptists.

They both sang in the church choir, and Pippin began

again to play the organ, perhaps with the exercise restoring some life to the wounded arm. He also played the mandolin, the guitar, and drum.

Horace and Ora Jennie lived together in harmony, often going off into the countryside to picnic and wander. They sometimes caught carp for their dinner in a nearby stream, a scene which Horace idealized later in his painting, FISHING IN THE BRANDYWINE. They liked good food and would feast on turkey at Christmas, goose on New Year's, and guinea fowl on birthdays.

Horace enjoyed the company of children and was often seen playing games with his stepson and the neighborhood youngsters. It is not clear why he and Ora Jennie had no children together. "They thought they were too old," some of the neighbors guess. Ora Jennie was thirty-six when she embarked on this, her third marriage, and Horace was thirty-two. Perhaps to make up for his own childlessness, Horace became a scoutmaster and led troops of boys on camping trips in the countryside.

It was a good life, and if it had not been for those sudden flashes of pain, and the constant struggle to recover use of his arm, Pippin might have been content. He would go to the Veterans Hospital in Philadelphia to see if the doctors there could not ease the twinges that damp weather always sent through his body. The steel plate that the French doctors had used to repair his shoulder was now a part of him. There was little they could do to help.

The war was constantly on Horace's mind, but he had no way to express his obsession. "One winter," he says in his autobiography, "I tried to write the story of my experience, but did such a bad job of it I gave it up." His mind returned again and again to the drawings. If only the pain in his arm would let up —if only he could find some way—

Nine years passed. Then one day in 1929 he began. Using his left hand he scratched a simple design with charcoal on the lid of an old cigar box. The surface was too small. There was nothing to hold the shapes. They rubbed off. He remembered the angry woman who had bought the doilies in Goshen.

Later that same year, watching the white-hot poker as it lay in the pot-bellied stove, he had a better idea. Holding the handle as firmly as he could in his stiff right hand, and balancing the rod on his knee, he took the extra leaf from the golden oak table, and with his agile left hand he maneuvered the panel against the smoking iron tip. It worked. And this time the design was there to stay, and bitten deeply enough to hold a color—the color black.

Black for the woods, the mysterious tracery of tree trunks, the shadow of night behind them, the horse and covered wagon, the single bent figure of a man—not riding, but himself guiding the animal through the storm —and now the footprints endlessly receding into the past, and out of the picture. White for the untouched surface of the wood, the virgin snow. He looked at it, saw the need for something to balance the wagon's black weight in the upper right, and added a willow log with twisted twigs toward the lower left. A lonely object, the log suggested the man's head rising above

62

LOSING THE WAY (1930) Owned by the Pennsylvania Historical and Museum Commission. Photograph lent by The Carlen Galleries, Inc., Philadelphia

the horse's neck, much in the way the tree trunks in the background repeated the pattern of bent legs, arrested movement, fatigue. With his poker Horace gave the burnt-wood panel a title in neat capitals at the bottom: LOSING THE WAY. Then he added his name, and a coat of varnish to make it look more like a "picture." His right arm felt better.

One day Horace got some oil paint and began to work on the picture "that was on my mind." He called it

THE END OF THE WAR: STARTING HOME (Color-plate 2, described on p. 51). His arm and shoulder were still weak and sore, and he could not work for long periods at a time. But he kept trying. In winter in the "second parlor" under a 200-watt light bulb, and in summer in his tiny garden, Pippin would sit, holding the wrist of his injured right arm in the fist of his left hand, thus controllong his motion to suit the tiny brushes and brush strokes with which he "advanced from side to side of the canvas."

He worked three years on his first canvas, adding at least a hundred coats of paint in his effort to achieve the feeling of the war—and no doubt to purge his memory of it. The very thickness of these layers of paint convey the bitter struggle in the mud, the blood and anguish that he could never put into words.

Ora Jennie was solicitous of Horace's need to paint, and the exercise it gave his arm. She would adapt her schedule to stay out of his way when he was working, provide conversation when the pain in his arm became so great he wanted to "rest for a while." If dinner was ready when he was deep in his work, she would quietly take the food away and warm it when he wanted it. When asked for her opinion of the picture, she would say, "That's nice," rather abstractedly, and hurry on to the real and important tasks of the day.

The entire neighborhood was aware that a change had come over Horace. "Mr. Pippin is painting," the neighborhood children would whisper, quickly abandoning plans to invite him into some game, and scooting away.

Even his friends learned to pause at the door instead

of barging in. "Pip—" they would call, waiting to see whether his enthusiastic voice would welcome them. If he were painting he would be silent, and they would know he really wished them to leave.

When the war paintings were completed, Pippin began to work on portraits. For one of his first subjects he chose his friend Paul Dague. Dague was the commander of the local Legion post and was later to become a member of the U. S. House of Representatives.

With a typically courtly gesture, Pippin presented the portrait to him as a gift, and Dague was rather embarrassed when his wife, no art lover, refused to have it in the house. The picture was turned over to the Legion Hall where the Legionnaires draped it in black. Dague's portrait stared at them with all the requirements of his office: insignia, buttons, medal, seal, and tiny gavel; the blue of his uniform against a canary yellow background. But Dague was a white man, and Pippin had given him a dead-white face—the face, so they thought, of a corpse.

Years later, when Dague donated the picture to the Chester County Historical Society, he either forgot the incident, or chose, because of his easy personal relationship with Pippin, to consider the white face not a racial statement but merely an element of design. The portrait, he wrote, was donated ". . . in the belief that it will thus be preserved for posterity as a symbol of the complete lack of racial consciousness which ever marked our long association together."

Another Legion friend to receive Horace's attention was Major General Smedley D. Butler. Butler, a Quaker, was a famous Marine Corps hero and commandant who had played a key role in the subjugation of black Haiti, but had later become an outspoken critic of "imperialist wars." In accepting the portrait Pippin painted of him, the general is said to have remarked jokingly: "But Horace, you left out one of my medals!" To which the artist answered seriously that he was distressed to hear it and would gladly do the picture over with seventeen, not sixteen, decorations showing.

How many drawings Pippin may have done and destroyed during this period no one knows. One "doodle" of Ora Jennie survives. It was evidently done in a doctor's office, while they were waiting their turn, for it is on a sheet of office stationery headed "History of the Case." It is a simple pencil sketch of a large woman seated in a rocker, with the perspective disturbingly tilted.

His formal portrait of Ora Jennie is a sober—almost cruelly sober—pyramid of plane geometry: the V of the face repeated in the V of the bodice. The cuffs are like periods to the collar. The chair's back complements the demurely parted hair, even to the terminal bumps. Hexagonal glasses dwarf the narrow eyes. Only the tiny watch provides an off-center note, though this is balanced by the lock of hair over the right eyebrow.

All of the early portraits are low-keyed. The subject is presented full-face or in profile, with little interest in characterization, but a great deal in pattern.

The least successful canvases of the period—THE MOOSE, MOUNTAIN LANDSCAPE, THE LADY OF THE LAKE —would seem to have been suggested if not copied di-

THE ARTIST'S WIFE (1936) From the collection of Richard F. Wade. Photograph lent by The Carlen Galleries, Inc.,
Philadelphia

rectly from life insurance calendars. This is probably also true of the pictures entitled BUFFALO HUNT, THE BLUE TIGER, ABE LINCOLN AND HIS FATHER BUILDING THEIR CABIN ON PIGEON CREEK, CABIN IN THE COTTON, CHRIST, and SQUIRREL HUNTER. But in each of the latter some corner of the painter's memory has come into play. trapping expeditions in the Poconos, the pattern of autumn leaves, a trip to North Carolina in 1925, his deeply religious spirit—with the result that the pictures come off.

Horace's eye was constantly casting about for subject matter, and, except for the "Victorian Interiors" to come, his first twenty-five oils examined most of the subjects he was to explore later on.

Of racial tolerance he spoke his piece in an early drawing: AFTER SUPPER: WEST CHESTER. The sketch for an oil that was to follow, it shows a Negro and white mother with raised hands touching lightly, in the common yard of their adjoining houses. The babies, on identical mats, are taking the sun. The children are playing together while the white grandmother is smoking her clay pipe as peacefully as any good black matriarch.

The finest and most "abstract" canvas of this period is the original BIRMINGHAM MEETING HOUSE, a picture that seems to reflect at once the artist's imminent stepping forth into the grand world of taste, tradition and unobtrusive wealth, and at the same time his quiet announcement of integrity. It says in effect: Here is your world but on my terms. Like so many of the later pictures this is a canvas both innocent and knowing, primitive and mature, simple yet subtle. It says again,

AFTER SUPPER: WEST CHESTER (1935) From the collection of Mrs. Arnold Gingrich. Photograph lent by The Carlen Galleries, Inc., Philadelphia

in its almost Puritan economy of grays, greens, and whites: Here is the best your world has to offer, as only I, with nature's help, can render it. The whites of the closed doors dominate the small patches of sky; the horizontal stones in turn are dominated by the vertical autumn leaves.

The stack of paintings was now beginning to mount at 327 West Gay Street, but Ora Jennie, as she bustled about, doing the laundry and trying to make ends meet, must have wondered of what use they could be. Horace's pension had been increased slightly—it would become $81.07 a month by 1944—but the cost of living had likewise risen.

Horace, in an attempt to justify his work, tried to sell the pictures for five dollars each, but only succeeded in raffling off one for one dollar. He then asked some of the white storekeepers, who were his friends, if they wouldn't consider taking a picture in payment of his accounts. Those who accepted probably did so more out of liking for Horace than out of any pleasure in the pictures, for no one in West Chester had a fresh eye for art, or considered Horace's painting anything more than a "hobby," or "an exercise for that injured arm."

Horace's barber took one of the paintings, BUFFALO HUNT, but his wife would not let him hang it. Later, when Horace's dealer offered the barber $75 for it, he was astounded. "I didn't believe anyone would be such a goddamn fool as to pay that for one of Horace's pictures," he told a friend, shaking his head. (Horace's dealer had already promised it to the Whitney Museum in New York for $150.)

In 1937, when the West Chester County Art Association held its annual invitation show, open to all comers, Horace entered two of his pictures, CABIN IN THE COTTON and ABRAHAM LINCOLN AND HIS FATHER BUILDING THEIR CABIN AT PIGEON CREEK. It was the first time a black man had ever brought a painting to the Association, and that fact made Christian Brinton, its

70

president, rather nervous. He was certain that this black artist would come to the opening, and he was worried about what the white members of the Association would say. Nor was he very confident about the quality of the two pictures. He confided these misgivings to John W. McCoy, a young artist who came by to help him hang the show the day before it was to open.

McCoy had married Ann Wyeth several years before, and was thus a member of the Wyeth family of painters who lived in nearby Chadds Ford. He had entered several of his own paintings in the show.

When he saw Horace Pippin's two pictures he was stunned. He rushed back to Brinton to tell him that they were "beautiful, true primitives!" He added that they were the best things in the show and that Brinton should bring them downstairs. Brinton reluctantly agreed to hang one picture beside the fireplace in the main room but left the other on the third floor. When McCoy's father-in-law, N. C. Wyeth, the famous illustrator, arrived shortly afterward, McCoy hurried to show him Pippin's pictures. The elder Wyeth agreed that they were very fine, and he lost no time in convincing Brinton that he should not only hang both pictures in a prominent place but that he should give the artist a one-man show later on.

Calling on the Pippins in Gay Street, Brinton inspected all of the artist's pictures and set about arranging a small exhibition. It contained ten paintings and seven burnt wood panels and opened June 9, 1937, at the West Chester Community Center.

Only one painting was sold. However, many people

came to see the show. Several women prominent in Main Line society invited the artist to tea and later bought pictures. Pippin reciprocated by painting one of them, Mrs. W. Plunkett Stewart, on her horse.

Holger Cahill, an art critic, and Hudson Walker, a dealer, were impressed by the pictures and borrowed four of them for a show which the former was helping to assemble for the Museum of Modern Art in New York. It opened in 1938, and in the catalogue, MASTERS OF POPULAR PAINTING: MODERN PRIMITIVES OF EUROPE AND AMERICA, the following words by the artist were quoted:

"*How I paint* . . . The colors are very simple such as brown, amber, yellow, black, white and green. The pictures which I have already painted come to me in my mind, and if to me it is a worth while picture, I paint it. I go over that picture in my mind several times and when I am ready to paint it I have all the details that I need. I take my time and examine every coat of paint carefully and to be sure that the exact color which I have in mind is satisfactory to me. Then I work my foreground from the background. That throws the background away from the foreground. In other words bringing out my work. The time it takes to make a picture depends on the nature of the picture. For instance the picture called *The End of the War, Starting Home* which was my first picture. In that picture I really couldn't do what I wanted to do, but my next pictures I am working my thought more perfectly. My opinion of art is that a man should have love for it, because my idea is that he paints from his heart and mind. To me it seems impossible for another to teach one of Art."

The exhibition included four of Horace's pictures. In addition to the one already mentioned by him there were: SHELL HOLES AND OBSERVATION BALLOON, CABIN IN THE COTTON and THE BLUE TIGER.

But the most important consequence of the Brinton show was that Pippin found a dealer. After the museum exhibition in New York, Hudson Walker took Pippin's paintings to his gallery at 32 East 52nd Street. Walker was unable to sell them, but Christian Brinton brought Robert Carlen, a Philadelphia art dealer, to see the pictures. Carlen was so enthusiastic that he offered to give Pippin a one-man show in his Philadelphia gallery the following year.

Forty-nine-year-old Horace Pippin—laborer, soldier, veteran, cripple—suddenly had a new identity. He was an artist.

When Pippin's first show at Carlen's opened in January 1940, it was an instant success. Art critics praised the work, and customers flocked to buy. Pippin, reading the reviews and noting the sales, smiled broadly. "The boys are doin' me good," he said. "The boys are doin' me good."

Carlen was not only able to sell the twenty-five paintings that comprised the show. He was the kind of dealer who took a personal interest in his painter's work, encouraging him, stimulating him to more ambitious projects, helping him to secure equipment and commissions, "talking him up" endlessly and contagiously.

Prior to the show the philanthropist Albert C. Barnes had happened into the gallery and seen Pippin's paintings lying face down on the floor. Intrigued by the colors which the cheap muslin had allowed to "bleed" through to the wrong side, Barnes asked that the pictures be turned right side up. He immediately bought five; and his assistant, Violette de Mazia, who accompanied him, bought the first of the BIRMINGHAM MEETING

HOUSE series. They reserved a seventh, CABIN IN THE COTTON, for the actor Charles Laughton.

Barnes had made his fortune manufacturing a patent cold remedy, Argyrol, before and during World War I. His first factory had been built in 1902 in a Negro section of Philadelphia, and thereafter Barnes had tried to identify with the black people who were his employees. He was now becoming known for his magnificent art collection, especially rich in French impressionist and post-impressionist painting, and for the "Barnes Foundation," where his theories of art were expounded, by Miss de Mazia among others.

Upon discovering Pippin, Barnes immediately suggested writing the introductory catalogue to Pippin's show. Carlen agreed. In his commentary Barnes stated: "It is probably not too much to say that he (Pippin) is the first important Negro painter to appear on the American scene and that his work shares with that of John Kane the distinction of being the most individual and unadulterated painting authentically expressive of the American spirit that has been produced during our generation."

Dr. Barnes invited Horace to see his collection at suburban Merion and to attend lectures being given there by Miss de Mazia. The understanding was that Pippin would not be obliged to pay for this privilege provided he attend the lectures for a year.

"Well?" Dr. Barnes asked, after showing Horace through the galleries.

"Very nice," the painter responded politely.

"But which do you like best?"

75

"That Renoyr . . . because they're full of sunlight . . . and look at them tits!"

Pointing to a Renoir on another occasion, Pippin told Miss de Mazia, "I'm going to take colors out of that man's painting and get them into mine." But he was critical of Matisse's high-key palette: "That man put the red in the wrong place."

Pippin did indeed sign up for the Tuesday afternoon classes but he attended only when he felt like it and for only a few weeks; and it may be doubted whether he understood at all the language of professional art appreciation.

"We do not teach students how to paint," Barnes had said of the lectures. "We teach them how to see." Horace could already see—and see with great personal insight—so it is hardly surprising that he sometimes dozed off during a lecture and snored.

Violette de Mazia remembers Horace as "very direct, very honest, and always attentive," but a fellow student who sat next to him recalls only his sleeping face and "an aura of sweat and whiskey."

Miss de Mazia talked about "unconscious distortions" and the "drama" of stark rhythmic beats—later comparing the use of these in Negro spirituals to Horace's insistent white doors and branch patterns in BIRMINGHAM MEETING HOUSE. She believes that Horace's WOMAN OF SAMARIA, painted during this period, owes something to a painting by the sixteenth-century Italian master, Tintoretto, in the Barnes Foundation. Actually the design of Pippin's picture appears to have been taken directly from an old book engraving found among the artist's papers after his death. The blood-red sky, according to Robert Carlen, was inspired by a sunset observed while crossing the Pulaski Skyway after Pippin's trip to New York for the opening of his third show at the Bignou Gallery.

Regardless of whether Horace at Merion was an eager devotee or a dozing captive, it cannot be denied that he acquired about this time a freedom in the use of color and a consequent liberation in design that were to extend his range and intensify his art. One need only compare his daringly successful PORTRAIT OF CHRISTIAN BRINTON, painted early in 1940, with the earlier portraits. The startling pale blue irises of the subject's eyes are picked up by the crescent pattern of the curtain and by two of the books. The white area in the lower right corner offsets the pallor of the face. The design of the handkerchief and necktie suggest something riotous but neatly folded and tucked away.

The formal portrait of his co-discoverer was painted from memory and presented to Brinton with gratitude —a gift coolly received, legend has it. Perhaps the local art critic sensed a note of mockery which the artist surely never intended, but which his artist's eye picked up, unconsciously but unerringly. Framed by his books, the scholarly connoisseur is just a little too well-dressed, well-posed, and thin-lipped to be getting the right vibrations. As we'd say today, he looks uptight.

The Bignou Gallery in New York was a chic establishment which sold the work of well-known Europeans. Horace's show there in October 1940 marked the first time that Bignou had given a show to an American.

A CHESTER COUNTY ART CRITIC: PORTRAIT OF CHRISTIAN
BRINTON (1940) Lent by the Philadelphia Museum of Art.
Given by Christian Brinton

78

The New York critics received the show with praise, greatly elevating Pippin's reputation. But only one picture, a small flower-piece, was sold.

Nonetheless, Pippin now walked in exalted circles. He was received by the wealthy, praised by the learned, flattered by the worldly. He met these people with an honesty and simplicity that endeared him to some but confused others. He is said to have deeply offended certain Negro painters who had received instruction by scoffing at art schools and academic technical standards. "To me it seems impossible for another to teach one of Art . . ."

Horace's patrons, the society women of the Main Line, invited him to have tea with them in their parlors. There is no reason to suppose that they weren't genuinely taken with his pictures and charmed by his personality, but there was an element of snobbism involved. Few of them had known an Artist in the flesh, and none of them had ever had occasion to entertain a workingman in their houses—and a black workingman at that. Horace had never felt that he was any man's inferior, but this was unfamiliar territory and he moved into it guardedly. Of the two parties, though, he probably felt more at ease than they did.

And he painted what he saw without inhibitions. Judging by Lilies, what impressed him most were the expensive potted plants, the intricately patterned Persian rugs, the old-fashioned doilies (antimacassars) then affected in such homes, the quantities of books in fine bindings, and the symmetry of the décor.

79

Some might detect a note of satire in the way he concentrated all this genteel opulence, and especially in the way he dis-remembered the neo-classical statuary as bathers taking off or putting on their undergarments, but this would be wrong. Horace had seen the raw materials for a new kind of picture, something that had never been seen from quite this angle—and he proceeded to put it together with his usual gusto.

There is also a memory of Goshen—of how the white man's well-stuffed drawing room must have looked to the furtive gaze of the colored laundress' son—in all these "Victorian Interiors" as Carlen was later to call them. The one that finally wound up in New York's Metropolitan Museum has the same magical, stupendously balanced "presence" as LILIES, though it lacks the enormous forked-tongue callas that serve as a "conductor" for all that riotous symphony of color.

A variation of this theme was THE DEN, which Horace painted for Jane Hamilton, wife of the (then) Chairman of the Republican National Committee. He gave it to Mrs. Hamilton as a "birthday surprise" following an afternoon in her manor house in Paoli. Horace is said to have absorbed a great many drinks while facing those leopardskin chairs and rows of china dogs, and later he kept calling up to ask which dog had which color hair, eyes, etc., so that the surprise gift was one of the worst-kept secrets in art history.

His memory, however, did not fail him in the exact gradations of texture. THE DEN's effect is achieved by contrasting the various patterns of skin, flagstone, and knotted wood with the texture of fine iron grillwork.

Horace was now often away from home. He moved in a world that Ora Jennie Pippin felt she could never enter. Ora Jennie had always been a shy woman, and the outside art world frightened her. She had never gone to one of Horace's openings in New York or Philadelphia, and now she did not go calling on the ladies of the Main Line.

She had always been necessary to Pippin—a homemaker, nurse, companion. She had even helped support him with her laundry. Now, she seldom saw him. He was either out with his friends, or shut in his room painting. The slim white women who would call for him in their big cars filled her with suspicion and fear.

Ora Jennie continued to take in laundry. Work had been the standby of her life. Of what use would she be without it? Anyway, how could she be sure that Horace's new-found success would last? And if it did, how much of this money would find its way into the family till? The clothes he had to buy, the trips he had to make, the oils and the canvases—! His success only meant more expense. She complained to neighbors that she never saw a penny of the money. Horace would fritter it all away in an evening, she said.

Ora Jennie looked into her mirror. Her 220-pound bulk stared back at her. Now that Horace no longer needed her, what would happen? She must lose some of that weight. There were pills, she had heard . . . pills that would keep her from being hungry. Pills that would make her slim.

No one knows how Ora Jennie Pippin managed to go from 220 pounds to 118 in those few short years. But her last months of life lead one to believe that she did indeed take pills—amphetamines. And with every pound she shed, she shed also, pill by pill, whatever remained of her peace of mind.

Meanwhile in the "second parlor" at Gay Street Horace was painting constantly.

There was to be another one-man show at the Carlen Gallery in March of 1941 and another at the Arts Club in Chicago in May. The Main Line ladies were clamoring for pictures. His audience was ready. He had only to produce. Whereas previously he had turned out three or four pictures a year, he now completed one every month.

He must have painted AMISH LETTER WRITER (Colorplate 5) to celebrate his unexpected success. It is one of his smallest pictures but it is full of happy surprises. Its orange tablecloth sings with joy—though the somber, bearded scribe hunched over his paper is much too busy making little scratches to notice. The oil lamp with its red wick and golden shade presides over a cozy family: pot, cup of coffee, and sugar bowl. The full moon, peeping through the small colonial panes in their lattice, nuzzles the writer's bushy hair. And behind him on the wall, like a sun in eclipse, the flat black hat on its unseen peg gives the masterful composition its resounding period.

CHRIST BEFORE PILATE and THE WOMAN TAKEN IN ADULTERY depicted biblical scenes with all the gay coloring of a county fair in June. It was the solemnity of posture and the grouping against architectural backgrounds that contributed drama to the familiar.

The catalogues for both shows carried a new introduction by Dr. Barnes who this time noted Pippin's use of "bright, exotic color for the depiction of objects and for the formation of compartmental patterns" and compared the artist's increasing expressiveness in the burnt-wood medium to Daumier and Cézanne.

But Barnes and Carlen had come to the parting of the ways. Barnes asked that he have first choice of *all* Pippin's future paintings, and Carlen, who envisioned a wider future for his painter, refused. Barnes left the gallery in a huff, proclaiming thereafter that Pippin was being "exploited" and "commercialized," and that he had painted no important pictures after leaving the Foundation. Years later, when Carlen took a friend to see Pippin's early work there, Barnes was still insisting that these were the "great" ones—and the choleric millionaire made Carlen wait outside on the sidewalk.

Carlen was no longer only Pippin's dealer. He had become his friend. Horace was so absorbed in his art that when he was not actually painting he wanted to spend his time *talking* about painting, or seeing other painters' work. He went more and more to visit Bob Carlen, and during the week he would write him postcards printed in capitals in a neat and beautiful hand. And he would phone him. "Collins!" he'd say, "I'm coming in Saturday. Will you have some money for me?"

Carlen would collect several hundred dollars, credited to past or future sales, and Pippin would be there late in the afternoon to receive it. He would spend hours in the gallery, talking and looking at other paintings.

It was very likely Carlen who suggested that Pippin go back to his roots to paint the John Brown trilogy, and it was at Carlen's that he saw one of Edward Hicks's many paintings of THE PEACEABLE KINGDOM. The colonial Quaker's painting must have been at least partly responsible for Horace's creation in the next few years of no less than four PEACEABLE KINGDOMS of his own which he entitled HOLY MOUNTAINS. But there was another cause.

In December 1941 the United States was plunged into the Second World War. Horace, who knew all of war's horrors, could not face another holocaust without some hope for the future. He had already painted his wartime memories, and now he wanted some affirmation that wars would not always exist. THE HOLY MOUNTAIN III (Colorplate 7) was that affirmation and Horace explained his picture with these words:

"My dear friends . . . It is the holy mountain, my Holy Mountain . . . The world is in a bad way at this time. I mean war. And men have never loved one another. There is trouble every place you Go today. Then one thinks of peace, yes there will be peace, so I look at Isaiah xi 6–10 and there I find that there will be peace. I went over it four or five times in my mind. Every time I read it I got a new thought on it. So I went to work. Isaiah xi, the 6th verse to the 10th gave me the picture, and to think that all the animals that kill the weak ones will Dwell together like the wolf will Dwell with the lamb, and the leopard shall lie down with the kid and the calf and the young lion and the fatling together . . .

"Now my picture would not be complete of today if the little ghost-like memory did not appear in the left of the picture. As the men are dying, today the little crosses tell us of them in the first world war and what is doing in the south today—all of that we were going through now. But there will be peace."

After talking with Carlen, Pippin would take his money and walk up the street to a restaurant-bar. There he would have dinner, order beer, and stand drinks for everyone in the place. Laughing and joking, boasting, and reminiscing, he would have a very great time. And when he got back to Carlen's a few hours later, the money would be gone.

Carlen would let Horace sleep for a while in the gallery. Then he'd walk him up the street to the railroad terminal and put him on the last train home—praying that the artist had sobered up enough not to fall off.

Ora Jennie had good reason to keep on with her laundry.

Pippin was now a famous man. Galleries all over the country were eager to have his work. He must have been tempted many times to forsake Robert Carlen. But he didn't. "He had such great integrity," Carlen says, "that he wouldn't leave me. He felt that I had given him his chance, and now I should share in his rewards."

Feeling that Philadelphia might not offer his painter enough opportunity, however, Carlen did make arrangements to share his work with the prestigious Downtown Gallery in New York. He also obtained for Pippin several commissions, including one to do an illustration for the Cotton Issue of *Vogue*.

Hollywood collectors were now vying with one another for Pippin's best work. Charles Laughton already had CABIN IN THE COTTON. Clifford Odets, Claude Rains, John Garfield, Edward G. Robinson, and others bought pictures. A Hollywood studio included him among twelve world-famous artists to paint the Temptation of St. Anthony for a film.

This turned out to be the largest but also one of the emptiest and least successful of his pictures. Horace used the layers of thin, streaky clouds he had painted so successfully in THE GET-AWAY, but here instead of tinging them with yellow to heighten the eeriness of the moonlit snow scene, he used orange to increase the unreality of the daytime vision. The Saint, apparently in sheep's clothing, reclines listlessly on a gray cliff over which the apparition of the Temptress looms—not too enticingly. Anthony is not looking at her, but at Death, a rather unconvincing scarecrow in the graveyard below.

Pippin was having his difficulties with the movie commission. He even wrote a letter of inquiry to the Pope, supposing that he of all men should be in a position to tell him what the Saint's temptations really had been. But when advised that His Holiness would be unlikely to respond in person to such a request, he took the advice of an intellectual acquaintance and laboriously plowed

86

through the Flaubert novel on which the screenplay was based.

Ellen Winsor, one of his Main Line patrons, remembers Pippin at that time: how he would silence the unbelievers among her friends with biblical stories "more poetic than anything in the Bible," and the "prophetic magnificence" of his presence among them. But the TEMPTATION looks like a Pippin without really being one.

Three little still-lifes were painted simultaneously with the huge pictures, and perhaps they were unconscious protests against that made-to-order commission with its portentous theme. FLOWERS WITH HAT AND CANE is a distillation of everything the artist had learned about his art. It is the central flower piece of the "Victorian Interiors" detached from their cluttered settings. The table-top is tilted toward the viewer as always, the better to set off the vase. The lace doily is enlarged the better to set off the drooping, sensuous flowers. The accessories—hat, cane and book—are drastically reduced in scale *but not eliminated:* to eliminate them, Horace correctly sensed, would reduce the still-life to mere decoration.

If his work was going well, Horace's life was not. His stepson, Richard Wade, had gone off to war, leaving a great emptiness in the big house shared with his wife.

Ora Jennie was not herself. She was restless and quarrelsome. She was resentful of Horace's absences and money-squandering, and as the neighbors remarked "she didn't bite her tongue."

She would wander around the house at all hours of the night, talking to her dead father, seeing visions. The weight-reducing "dope" had taken its toll. She no longer took any interest in cleaning the house or making meals, and when Richard returned home on leave she hardly recognized him. Worst of all she was obsessed with the idea that Horace had other women. She refused to leave his side when there was another woman in the house.

One night in March of 1946 she threatened Horace and a young girl, the daughter of one of their friends who had come to visit. She ran up the stairs and began tearing up clothing and blankets. When Horace tried to quiet her and give her some medicine, she refused to take it, saying it was poisoned.

Two doctors came to see Ora Jennie and both recommended that she be committed.

On March 18, 1946, Horace tenderly put her in his car and drove her to the Norristown State Mental Hospital. Ten days later he drove back to tell the doctors all that he could that might help in her treatment. He asked to be called when she was well enough to come home.

Horace was now out of the house even more than before. He would put in a night of drinking at Little Joe's place on the corner, order "submarine" sandwiches and a round of drinks for everyone within earshot, and then (no matter what the hour and as loudly as possible) announce that he must phone his dealer, and confer importantly with Bob Carlen over the subject and material to be used in his next picture.

Night after night he would come in after midnight. Falling into bed, he would sleep until late the next day. On Friday night of July 5, 1946, there was some talk that the refrigeration at Little Joe's had broken down, spoiling the food, but Horace went nevertheless and stayed drinking even later than usual.

The next day at 3:45 in the afternoon his housekeeper, Mrs. Pearl Hairston, wondering why he was not yet up, went to his room but was unable to rouse him.

Horace Pippin was dead.

His death certificate records only that on July 6, 1946, at the age of fifty-eight, his heart stopped. A funeral was held at the Day Funeral Home in West Chester, and he was buried there in Chestnut Grove Annex Cemetery.

Two weeks later, without being told of his death, Ora Jennie Pippin died at Norristown State Hospital.

Four paintings were left unfinished in the Pippin living room. These last pictures are somber in treatment and subject matter. Without a trace of his usual affirmative disposition THE PARK BENCH, the last picture he finished, is a great one. Is it far-fetched to consider it a psychological self-portrait—the study of a man who has achieved great success only to find himself at the end poorer and more alone than he had ever been before? Others might consider it to be the artist's only clear statement about the black man's exclusion from white America. It shows a Negro in ill-fitting work clothes, one hand in his pocket as if resigned to unemployment, the other grasping the back of the bench as if about to force the resigned body into action. The unhappy face suggests both thoughts. And the background of black shadows between ranks of leafy trees is relieved only by a white squirrel contentedly chewing on a nut. Propaganda for a worthy cause? Or the universal human condition? As with so many of the great paintings of Goya or Daumier, you can take your choice.

Clifford Odets, who once owned THE PARK BENCH, said: "The effect of the picture is of an insane, fixed glare; of deep despair."

On the easel in the Pippin living room was a sketch for another HOLY MOUNTAIN—one quite unlike the others. Horace had just begun to lay in the blue sky and gray rocks beside a blasted tree. A lion, a panther, and a wolf are in the foreground. The second world war was over now, and in this final version of a favorite subject the artist was surely preparing to convey a less optimistic message. The landscape is stripped of verdure. There is no place for tanks to maneuver, nothing on which to drop bombs this time. The bald mountain is split by an ugly fissure. The three ghostly carnivorous animals are accompanied by no human figures. After Hiroshima an urgent warning must have seemed more appropriate than a vision of paradise.

During his lifetime Horace had painted many visions. "He wanted to paint remembered scenes," the art critic Frederick C. Wight wrote, "but he wanted still more to paint imagined ones. He was a dramatist and poet with his brush."

90

THE HOLY MOUNTAIN IV (1946) From the collection of
Mrs. Arnold Gingrich. Lent by The Carlen Galleries, Inc.,
Philadelphia

Of his earlier HOLY MOUNTAINS Horace himself had
said: "If a man knows nothing but hard times he will
paint them, for he must be true to himself, but even that
man may have a dream, an ideal—and 'Holy Mountain'
is my answer to such dreaming."

91

THE AUTHORS

Selden Rodman, poet, biographer, art critic, historian, and anthologist, initiated and directed the famous mural paintings by Haitian primitive painters in the Cathedral Ste. Trinité at Port-au-Prince. His 1946 monograph on Pippin was the first book ever written about a black artist. The most recent of his books are *The Caribbean, The Mexico Traveler* and *South America of the Poets.* His wife, Carole Cleaver, is a former editor of *Mademoiselle* and *The Wyckoff News.* They live with their children in Oakland, New Jersey.

THE HOLY
MOUNTAIN III